Odd Bloom Seen from Space

Winner of the Iowa Poetry Prize

University of Iowa Press, Iowa City

Odd
Bloom
Seen
from
Space

Timothy
Daniel
Welch

University of Iowa Press, Iowa City 52242
Copyright © 2017 by Timothy Daniel Welch
www.uipress.uiowa.edu
Printed in the United States of America

Design by Ashley Muehlbauer

The University of Iowa Press is a member of Green Press
Initiative and is committed to preserving natural resources.

Printed on acid-free paper

Library of Congress Cataloging-in-Publication Data
Names: Welch, Timothy Daniel, 1976– author.
Title: Odd bloom seen from space / Timothy Daniel Welch.
Description: Iowa City : University of Iowa Press, [2017]
| Series: Iowa poetry prize | Includes bibliographical
references.
Identifiers: LCCN 2016040305 | ISBN 978-1-60938-504-0 (pbk)
| ISBN 978-1-60938-505-7 (ebk)
Classification: LCC PS3623.E4637 A6 2017 | DDC 811/.6—dc23
LC record available at https://lccn.loc.gov/2016040305

for Tana Jean—

are we funny
with magic beans?

Contents

Acknowledgments

Thankful acknowledgment is given to the following journals in which the poems first appeared: *Green Mountains Review Online*: "The Children"; *Best New Poets 2012*: "On the Isle of Erytheia"; *Rattle*: "Bolero."

Thanks to the many readers and supporters whose insight helped shape this book, including my friends at San Diego State University, Florida State University, the Juniper Writing Institute at Amherst, and the Port Townsend Writers' Conference. I am especially indebted to the University of Wisconsin–Madison Institute for Creative Writing for the fellowship and the supportive faculty, in particular Ron Wallace, Sean Bishop, and Amaud Jamaul Johnson for their unwavering faith in my work. Thanks to my family: Lynn, Mary, Ron, Karen, Krystal, and Natalie. Thanks also to teachers and mentors Ed Kleinschmidt Mayes, Rebecca Edwards, Sandra Alcosser, Marilyn Chin, Wanda Coleman, Glover Davis, Sharon Bryan, Matthew Zapruder, Carl Phillips, Diane Roberts, and Andrew Epstein.

I am indebted to poet Craig Morgan Teicher for being the judge my wife kept promising was out there.

Special thanks to fabulous friends Kara Candito and Erin Belieu, who broke my poetry heart when I needed it, refastened it, and each time gave new life to my work.

Thank you, Keith Leonard, Matthew Modica, and Asako Serizawa for your inspiring devotion to these poems.

And thank you most of all Tana Jean Welch, my intergalactic lover.

You're on Earth. There's no cure for that.

—S. Beckett

1

On the Isle of Erytheia

My virginity, like a herd of red cattle
                I drove for seventeen years,

was dumb and almost

        beautiful—
           I spent my time tending

to the animals in me. I remember their tails,
                those tender curls, and

      the long nights
following strays to the rim

           of town and faltering, spooked

              by a train whistle or the start
of an engine. Some place, this

Erytheia, for skinny boys
          without a sense of butchery—

a tiny island of Greek heroes
who came to kill whatever

        sad, hoofing creatures insulted

the gods. Then the myth

of my own hard slaughter: there was
        a girl, she led me to a vacant life

guard tower, told me to begin with the shirt
        or the pants, my inadequacy was

a Homeric round-up.

Against the silver-rooted water
    the sky reddened

     and blackened itself, a little
breeze crept calmly along

    the sand and dropped grain
        after grain into its golden bowl.

Nose of Least Comparison

I have a nose the Greeks might call
their own,
        or the Tunics, a great gnomon

    leaning in the sun
like a timepiece casting shadows
            on a garden stone.

      This is my grandfather's nose—

who came from Greece during the Second World War,
        a fugitive from his family

unable to carry out his mother's decree
    to kill his unmarried sister who went
        with the postal clerk, got pregnant, and

disappeared from Patras to one of the Ionian
        islands.

A ripple   to his ripple,
is there a story to each wave that crosses the sea?

How is it history has come
                        and gone yet for the worried face
we place on it, a face nosing above

growing ecological disasters; a face
            of concentration treading the floodgates

of Bangladesh and tsunami ravaged
        Japan. By night, the tower of my face

            rises in search of its
architectural antecedents supporting the black rims

        of my spectacles,

            and from that height I'm a glacially
whittled valley, or a lost city

        as a tower of Carthage articulating
the capital building before its—twice—ruin

            of salt and fanatics, before inclusion

        in UNESCO, before Tunisia.
            A tower belonging to the historic drama

it provides, the feature from which sailors

watched seaward cargos of cumin, cinnamon,
sumac, foreign

mercenaries hauling elephants
on Roman triremes, the harbor master

counting slave girls and horses,

and fleets of parading cannons
tilting on an eastern breeze.   This is

my grandfather's nose—a man

who found his dishonored sister
hiding with the clerk,
but it was too late,   the child

had already been born. And before
he could raise a casserole dish

to collapse her skull,
he caught a glimpse of his profile

on the infant, held up

the child indelicately, and stayed for dinner.

Tell the Truth But Leave Immediately After

Like the bear constellation who—after eating
        the horse—gets hitched
                to the wagon and

learns the difficult way that honesty is a kind of
solitude,   a little shade of tree and
the hint of feet going—

                I have lived most of my life alone.
But not entirely. There was a time when a man

solicited me for sex but first wanted to buy me
        new shoes, so we window-shopped

until evening. The next step was to try on
"a dark boot," he said, and I remembered how

I wondered about the *soul* on my way home from school or
naked, touching a window smudge of a hand with
my hand, not knowing

what side of the glass I was on, or where
I was, where I was going, a soul in halves, an organ
like the spleen that listens
      and adjusts its white pulp—

I wanted a truth that blistered and
if possible said something about
my place in a brutal commerce,

my place in avoidance and so completely
wake from a dream like the one in high school when
I knew I loved
one of two twins—Julie, not

Jenny—with such clarity I poured orange juice
in my cereal. When I asked Julie if she'd go out

I left wondering which is more
human, to shoot
or to be shot, and if there's any truth

to taking a punch—close your eyes and
smile? or if the old Slovenian proverb,

     "Tell the truth but leave immediately after—"

       asks to live one's life alone,
like the man standing outside a shoe store
watching his young prospect run—

because if a truth is ever told then
no one can ever leave.

You must discover the landscape as you go.

—Lawson Fusao Inada

The Children

The snow was falling on the beach
and so the children

gathered it
                    into their hands.

They mixed white sand and whiter frost

into balls of light
            and threw them. I watched

a girl's eye drift naked among the tide.
I watched the evening give way

to the boulevard.

                    And when the snow moved
inland, I became scared

for them, of how this will seem
in memory,   if this was happiness,

and if it were me, what might this

      have meant. How unreal

seems a child's mind, these brief comets
smoldering

            at my feet.

Seal Beach

The sea is flimsier than I remember, not as dark,

              not as deeply.

        Maybe I've aged well, or aged enough

to see beyond its shore. The tiny town where I was raised,
                my childhood Pacific,

                it's been years but I headed west
and the sight of it in pieces

            spilling itself into place—this *oceanic*,
one of those words that breaks

against itself. And to swim
               the ghost currents of Seal Beach,
       looking for shells like lenses to enlarge the sea.

But the seashells of a boy are not the bones of a man—

               and seals surely
held their bones here once, lifting their backs

upon the water like the town pier on its wooden beams,
        its 50s diner and the teenage waitress

                I'd meet after her late shift to stroll
the full length of the pier. Distances were longer
        then, my heart

leaner as we passed fishermen who paused to glimpse
                her skirt, their hooks

sinking into that stillness. For years I was haunted
by those summers cooled by the sand, the pier

        lamped at dusk when I'd see her, a bright fissure—

and when the pier collapsed it was rebuilt
                above the ruins like an obsessive

        question: on what do we prop our lives and
                what if it can't hold?

        I've changed the way I love because of this

and built my relationships far from shore like the pines
        that support themselves by an earthen stem—

I've climbed them
                and wavered at the top. I've had to fall

to feel a flash come over me
                worn hard as water.

Parts of a Feather

—*It is surely cohesive.*

G. Stein

In my searching there's the vane, rachis, barb,
afterfeather, and
hollow shaft—

built up from small drifts and
counterturns, an explanation of outer patience
suggests if I had feathers, a gull

or an owl would suit me
because my silence, my satisfied
helplessness, is either tucked tightly

in a sheen, or widely spread. What I know
of wings—of how arms break
to be held—is the way the feather

intersects with itself and its
others, macroscopically, shifting but
entwined. The rotten feather

is smoothed, oiled, or pulled and when diseased
can be constrictive, stunting
like fear from a young age, a chronic

necrosis. How many feathers
does one need to pull to line
the nest, asleep and adrift

like the river in Northern California—some distance
from Reno—called the Feather, fed by
the Sierra Nevadas

as it turns each season toward
the Rio Grande. As a skinny boy,
with some urgency,

I'd fish there, then swim if
it was summer, float
to where the river flared

into catfish, crawdad, rainbow or brown
trout. There's an easiness
in the way its feathers became divisions

along its shore: mornings
as the sunlight drove the fish
to bite, my father might break

open a beer as early as nine and
teach me to thread night crawlers on
hooks. There was no more silence

in him than that river refracting
the early mountain shade, no more calm
than a stone tossed to wobble

the edges of the boat. When I go back
along the spine, the bristles
that crisscross the short branchlets

become clearer, a single feather shows
itself to be a system, each quill
its own feather within a feather—

after my father's second divorce
he began listening to Robert Bly's audio tapes
and growing a beard. He opened

the door to the Lincoln to drive me
around the neighborhood and promised
that we would break the cycle

of shame began by his father—the eagle, vulture,
baby bird—and his father before him.
What a sad perch, the dark

twists in the bone so sincerely
connected to the strings from which
we fly, loving and dying monsters

crested with barbs. But then we
learned the river, caught
our share of fish, which was enough,

and which we scaled together,
gutted, and then ate. Each frightening
wing of me eats and eats because

I can never know what's holding me up,
or feel the stiff plumes
or the sick broadening.

For my colleague, I have an interest—

Of his stomach and the shirt that stretches there
    there isn't enough shirt

Of his beard two-fingers past his chin the man
    is Walt Whitman

Of his Halloween invitation to visit a haunted house
    in Chicago, is he serious?

I am not
    though of his invitation I am considerate

And of his five children I know of only Becky—
    college-age, like one of his students

And of his students there is a baffling sincerity, they
    like him fine—and between us

There is silent competition for the adoration
    of the student populace

But of my children there are none but students
        and an amaryllis I water with a measuring

Cup—cold water, about as cold as I can pour it
        and I can be cold to my students

And drip cute insults, and they laugh though
        there is a price for humor

There's remorse, wondering if it was bad
        to tell a student he speaks as well as he writes

When his subjects disagree with his verbs
        and of the streets there are a thousand

And a million grammatical errors—that's why
        I love my colleague's teaching style,

The plain way he color codes his lessons on
        the white board—his penmanship is like a woman's,

Purple, and slightly looping into a series of quarries
        such as What is a claim?

What is a Reason? What is a refutation?
        What is a concession?

I try to make my students ask these questions
        themselves, but how can they seriously ask

Themselves Who modernized
  the Argumentative line of reason?

A question I have asked myself many times and
  still don't know the answer—

But to communicate this to my students, to ask
  a question that they can't answer

And to know it or not know it, but to answer anyway—
  ah, my friend, we mustn't be coy

With knowledge. That should come first. Next
  should be people. It's strange to connect

The two together and of my greatest students
  I think of bodies of water filling

And shifting out of the shadows—they are lucky
  if they can take the shape the world

Has dug for them. So, my colleague and I meet
  around lunch time, and he speaks in dissertation,

Says more about Star Wars than anyone I've ever known,
  and asks me again if I like Chaucer.

Star Wars and Chaucer. Katy Perry and hygiene.
  Our students and ourselves.

Slobs of the Ineffable Go to Evensong

1.
Frank is a walk made strange, made Spaceman,
made all the more interesting baked
with his magic light lunchbox in the English
department lavatory—

2.
of all the pot he's had today, of all
the chicken, my friend, on Tuesdays, we
are the descants of obsession, of design, and as poets
we've schooled-up to see ourselves even more

3.
arcane. Our friendship is based on opera,
Fellini, and garage bands. We get bored
into things and suffer till
we're bored, till Frank says something

4.

inappropriate like *what's it like having*
such a fuckable wife?—
I think understanding him means
wanting what he wants, his taste in songcraft:

5.

I like it when the singer is indecipherable
so it's easier to sing along. But Spaceman on
the lawn, on the wooden deck with a burger—
he moves like David Hasselhoff stepping from a rocket

6.

and flirts—*A fully comprehensible erection and a body left out*
in the shine, Timothy you are a poet capital P. Whatever you touch
maxes itself out in me like a MasterCard. I suppose
what hinges on contrition, on mania or nonsense

7.

becomes friendship as much as illusion, but
in absolute disinterest he says, *come to Evensong,*
come to the service and I'll sing to you
from the choir. For Frank the fall furthers

8.

the flight, and love spills innumerably
at loose distances while the church
bears us. It's strange how he's Christendom
in immense clothes, in cassock and surplice,

9.

wafting white sleeves that blur and fade, and
piped from the organ a kind of light
that bruises the old men sitting upon
some great assumption, the obscured eyes

10.

from the pews where, half-full, the church
listens to Nicolas de Grigny and I go looking
toward the vaults and rafters—
have I fallen from   am I going to   whose spirit

11.

have I heard—until I'm back to St. John's
Episcopal Church that seems to shine upon a dead word:
Welkin. It used to mean a curved sphere like a movie
screen where philosophers, poets, and saints believed

12.

the night sky—its stars and dusts as incense swung
on silver chains—was projected, evidence that heaven
is a reflection, even Frank who hangs his own image by
the shoulders and is nothing but orbital, enameled,

13.

perfecting what's real by eyeing me from across
the church and wondering who I am,
if my ancestors sang and schemed as celestial
bodies, if they believed in a welkin that could

14.
make their intimacies worthwhile. I look at Frank
and realize the artifice that there's no welkin
in the 21st century, which is why he is so needed,
why some of my ancestors were born while

15.
docking the Mayflower, and why these Quakers
were martyred. We are a species of enchantment
and tempt history in our spasms while Frank
sings, wishing October would last where nothing

16.
augments. He loosens the cope and takes me out
to the churchyard to share a joint;
farther off the children's choir looks—
looks nothing like children.

The Odd Bloom of Sept. 11, Seen from Space

The astronaut said
it was an *odd bloom*, smoke from a wound

at the base of the column
          streaming south of the city.

I don't know
     how to collect each new

          perspective, but I lived
in the garage of a Vietnamese

bachelor then. I was told to use the kitchen
     whenever. I had carpet and

my own side entrance passing six garbage
cans, and the garage door

     was lined in mirrors
so that I could see the television and my own face,

peripherally, which is what this is, some side-line

  reflection, because if memories
gain distance, then they are seen anew.

It's been over ten
     years since 9-11, since I slept

in the garage that I decorated with water
color paintings of red skies, red bodies of water,

  and pools of yellow
moons seen through branches; the paintings

were a blur of quick smudges of men
  and women walking on a bridge

strung with gas lamps. There are odd

blooms whenever I think back on my twenties,
and the solitary evenings when

I could hear my landlord and
    his girlfriend talk, too hushed

to translate their affection, even if I knew how,
and when I needed something to eat, I'd walk

  behind the couch they were on
so I might toast some bread. From here

I can almost see that astronaut.
He is married; he has an apartment with a pool;

and he paints a blue sphere
where waves, moment to moment, return

the thousands silently, as if breaking
free of orbit together.

Containment

The last evening of three
days in my robe when

      neighbors doing it
with the windows open broke

my lethargy—I could feel the universe
like an inkling, the passage

of time parting
open at the neck, revealing the portal

to a revelation that I am ripe
      with sloth. Self-made promises

are the chili bowls
on the bedroom floor I stepped

over all week, but since Tuesday
      even a rotting dish makes
its own logic. I must

try to make it better, do something in
the kitchen—

      I looked, thought of the neighbors'
hysteria, there was too much all
at once.

Then the stove light, flickering painlessly, not even
yellow—

I will come to you, stumbling, burned
out, with this other bulb.

Outside Los Banos, California

I'm no authority on horizons,

the beginning and end
     made dark by rat feet in graindust,

       the sky
          a roasting lamb, the great

nameless comet catching
     the deer's sleep—

I'm no authority on the highway, its animus
of engines, the spasms
         of orange-blaze

     on manzanita hills, rolling weeds, fire

weeds, violent tones
      like crackling glass—

I'm not even sure how to reach my
     destination: the one image of my father

who came home after his stroke to
        the lights on, windows

open, letting the insects in—how he stood holding
his shoe to swat

                the mosquitos and phantom

midges, and how they scattered
when he shook

        the lampshade. There's a brutal distance

                between men. I feel it in the landscapes
                        I've crossed,

or too afraid to cross, how
                my father, among the flies, reaches

out and I feel the interstate
        between us, and how, after

                I've made it so
                        far, he asks me what is killing

him—

        I point back, as if to give
            directions.

O pale-eyed Form,
The victim of seduction

—S. T. Coleridge

2
Bolero

These Arrow-Smitten Stymphalian Birds

It's a sad thing to fly too low.

The summer sends its creeping greens
            under the window—

                robins, brown and red,
divide the moment at hand into beautiful

          blood piercings.

I've been at it most of my life—the table,
flamenco, the scented

smoke, my corkscrew staccato, castanets
ornamented with

                momentary firebirds.

To Laura, a Virgin-Unwed

That beard you grew in your dream—so long
you tripped on your way to the plaza—grew
and grew, got twisted in your pilsner, slapped the goulash
at the café in Malá Strana, then crooked
round your neck, covered your chest, and leaning
toward me, you cried on it. In the morning
you wanted to know what it meant and I
couldn't say. "Does it mean that I'm a lesbian?"
you asked, "But I've never *been* with anyone.
I'm saving myself for the Peace Corps." Sex wasn't,
but sometimes was, what drove Emily Dickinson
to the little white dress, or Sir Isaac Newton's
fondling of the spheres, or Nikola Tesla's Death
Ray Machine which was a huge phallus coil
rippling and vibrating across the dunes. They
were thought to have died virgins because love
grows bristles, grows in the way of the thing
that became them, maybe, or they were afraid,
or pious. But you are here now studying
in Prague, and you need it to become a part of you,
on your face and deep enough to echo through

the bohemian forest. Maybe the dream means
you are becoming a tourist of the flesh? Tell me
what could be more plain than walking through
the castle gardens passing statues of green, copper
gods? When you read Catullus, do you want
anything? Does it hurt to imagine a book of poems
catching fire in the afternoon as if to lose
your own pluck? Do you need to prove
you are alive to me, or anyone? I could ask you
to fuck me to prove it, but what for? So take
a moment to look around, how the peacocks brandish
their feathers but do not fly, how the clouds
descend yet incapably cool our shoulders. The world
descends and descends along dry rock, unwinds
and unwinds to the castle garden as a way to rearticulate
Saint Starosta the Sorrowful, forced into marriage by
her father the king and, refusing the pagan prince, grew
a hideous beard. She was crucified as the patron saint
of unhappily married women. How hard
she prayed to be ugly, to be undeserving and
undesired, how embarrassed she was of nude Apollo
watching her soak her crotch in the fountain.

Owls

Owls and their Michael Jackson
hooting in the trees, eyes

snow-burned with light, predators of the very
small, and fluttering like
Michael Jackson in his castle for children—

How am I ever to know those gods, feathered satellites
watching years go by, long years since *Thriller*
and the world stranger, imaginative,

technological and
Michael Jackson's sperm, his silver
glove

gone? There's beauty in wanting more
time to be young, to sing and seize it in a photograph or
music video before it goes from us—

but that's the occult of time, and I'll have
only as much as I can leave behind in late July,

when the movement of trees are
beginning, the field is beginning, the roots
of vines cluster into white vetches,

darting to where the ivy deepens
and singes by evening. I listen to *Thriller*,

fall asleep on the seafloor
of images and awake to the feeling there's no

animal left in me, so when the owl calls
      I go out—
I walk to where the young blackberries

redden beside blue pines, they are berries
at the bitter age, small, they have been promised

fountains. I'm not something that breaks
into electrons from birdcall, but the circuitry goes looking
in order to be

seen. A lonely child of ten siblings, Michael Jackson dropped
to the middle of the floor and became.

Look at me now, whatever you are—
I am the river of my life and a frog stammers, a squirrel
clucks, a hot wind

buries my face in a beach
of black sand

and within it the moon.

"I don't want to die on a listserv"

for K. C.

I was walking with a friend

who spoke of her lover—a Peruvian sculptor—
and how they carry on

through internet sex.
"It's strange," she said,   "sex without odor."

I could sense the north county in its ritual
controlled burn—

she turned to me and asked,
"Why don't we lie down? So I can think of him."

Together we were like reading *Anna Karenina*
on a Kindle or watching a silver titmouse

fluttering

its smoky wings

and rubbing its beak on a branch

                    as its own text.

There was strangeness
        in her touch,

                almost insurmountable space

           between megapixels,

un poco   *un poco.*

What graceful Absences (to borrow a certain poet's phrase) are haunting those windows.

—T. W. Higginson

Retractable by Design

after *Fog Horns* by Arthur Dove, the first "extractionist" painter

1.

the fog horn is heard tho the horn itself is not seen is how pink ovals come to
    resemble a uterus

2.

its sound inks thru a low cloud and Dove paints it the same as steam, mist,
    glaucoma in a cornea

3.

wherever his marbles dangle so does the sun or moon, and the stars are marbles
    but smaller

4.

are the marbles angry? are they finally at peace? do marbles roll toward or from
    the pain of others?

5.

on the sheet music notation takes form, cosmic embryos sound more
        brightly than trees

6.

what is the fog to resemble without the horn? before jazz there was
        something called jas

7.

before abstract painting there was extractionism, gravity, a mighty
        light we are born into

Portraits at the Funeral

1.
It was a closed casket, a sky

shut-in. We stood, shaded
where she was buried, the sunlight held

the hill.

2.
      I have no other word for death

but *dammit.* My father took it hard—
he lifted his camera to his mother's casket,
said, "Cheese,"

then turned to the portrait of the deceased
arranged with fuchsias and pointed lilies:

Mary,
hands at the piano

and wearing the blue dress her mother
sewed, this portrait taken in 1938 when

she was sixteen. My father told everyone
she was never sixteen.

3.
After the funeral, he walked through
Mary's house

and I wanted to frame him there,
the tired dog at his feet, the empty halls, the mirrors

covered in black cloth. I imagined the violence-turned-grief
of his boyhood confronted and
confused.

4.
 I once asked Mary what made him
go bad. She said she didn't know, but
he was always like that. Some horrible
maw was at him like Prometheus on

the Caucasus mountains, black with asphaltum, audience to
but out of the reach of the chains,
a kind of ancient theater

for the feathered thing that ate his liver and that he
confused for a mate. Who could intercede?

5.
She painted everything on her approach
to nothing. The bright vermillion
mesas and creosote of New Mexico, the burnt lakes
where the Sierras overturned the sky,

and these landscapes hung
on her walls like portals, charms
dipped in oil. No one at the funeral
mentioned the Alzheimer's or

how she began erasing
herself. How it first started with white
paint and the bucket standing
in the bathtub. Everyday she'd give a little

brush stroke, painting over her landscapes,
until, moment to moment,
one could not decipher the wall
from the work.

6.

        But then my father was glad

I didn't get to see her erased, getting thin, refusing
to be photographed, eating nothing, drinking Sprite.

And when she slept, he photographed her hand, her sleeping face—
at dinner my father said, "This was her hand."

Silver

I have questions: at the drive-in
when your father opened the Coors Light from

the cooler and poured it on
your head, was it meant to quiet you?

was the shock?
was it meant to pool as long

as this: twenty years with some
kind of back pain? and now the acupuncturist

turns the harp with needle
upon needle through the neck

moves the *qi* as body sap
through a Sitka spruce and she asks

whether your father sat
you down on blocks of ice

for long periods of time to
make such blue in the deep body—

Do you know to straighten a reed
you must bend it farther back, sometimes

so far it shivers as you are now,
clattering, and this,

      the way you are with tenderness
when there is yelling?

Self-Portrait of a Sister, Cubist-Style

At evening, the houses captioned with light,

and from above the slanted roofs spilling
upward and back, my young
sister stands,
                              points her toe.

And conceding the witch-angles of
youth, the awkward stubble, the grass and
wind—as a fly encircling the pepper tree,

or a wren's tail thrust in
panic mirrors a restless, hurried dance—
standing there my sister
                              points her toe.

One small and leafy gesture like unfolding wet
paper among rose blossom,
and the yard silvery from coastal

air where the neighbor's fence rising against
bougainvillea hangs, and of a hundred,
one thorn intersecting the nearest

fragment of sky, faintly
and quiescently upon her extended
neck, the evening's single focus halts

                              at the edge of her foot.

She seems to have grown while I was away. Leaving at an abrupt moment
and returning to another, changed, with

changed attention, her shinbone
pronounced, her ankle's knot

shivering like an anchor becoming suddenly

                                 part of the wave.

I was away too long, long enough to know
how the glass on a London bank becomes indifferent to light,

and long enough to have been hungry, and wandering,

learning charity by giving it, stupidly dropping
my last quid into a violin case in
the underground;

and modesty, for what it's worth, and possibility—

thinking we inherit beauty by discovering it for ourselves,
or by the search, or a little suffering;

                           and I wanted beauty.

So I left the white city as I found it, the Queen's gardens
dressed in purples,

and the steps at St. Paul's rising to columns, and columns to dome
concentrating on a point above me; but what point?

When the airplane began to rise it seemed the clear passage back
            was up
                        and with wings,

and when I finally landed I felt as though I had been moving, just
moving, and home
            I moved more deliberately.

As the sun shadows the small yard
of our California home, and crabgrass
                        staggers in fits of green,

the white legs of my sister sway for a moment and stop, white legs
upon which she had shed her childhood,

and holding her place in the yard
                        points her toe.

People Are Taking Advantage of It

In today's world, abortion
is like having a new pair of underwear—

      or says a student paper.
It's like a toupée the mercurial heart

questions, but whose, but which?
      My sister got one the other day—

a new pair of underwear—and then wiped
the sink with the dirties.

When she had her abortion, she kept it
      from me, hidden

      until our father left for China to sell
Water Baby Dolls, then

she told how the young nurse held and
      rocked her side to side, saying *that's*

a dear, that's a dear.

The Hot Siberians

Chekhov told Olga
that if a story begins with seduction
it ends in forced prostitution;

if it begins with marriage then
it ends in a miscarriage; or

if a tale begins with the heart, then
it will certainly

end.
Chekhov had a thing with guns, too.

When he put on his coat, there was a rattling
of shells; when he removed his coat, a stray

bullet might roll onto the floor.
Olga once

slipped the rounded tip into
her cleavage. He called this

repetitive designation. If a bullet was seduction,
a perfect bullet could marry

the heart in a shock of light. For the most part

guns are only props
until the third act—

simply follow the bullets down the stairs, or the rifle
missing from a bookshelf—

at some point our backs are
against a wall,

we're staring down a blue barrel knowing

if we weren't going to die
then we wouldn't have bought a ticket.

                        Olga needed love so

she focused on it, she would spend
the afternoon in Chekhov's coat

moving as February moves,
as he might have moved along

            the Taganrog Bay. Or how Olga moved

wearing nothing
but his coat. With the buttons opened

to the room he tears at the sleeves
so it floats bodiless to her feet, soaking

        with lantern light

swinging from the crossbeam. One or
two shadow-selves reenter from

backstage. She has come to him.

His hands are freezing. She says *Put them here.* The rain

fills the cemetery with Rimsky-Korsakov, with the music
of headstones. She lets him

warm himself with the cold
underneath. And the coat passes
between them, bulging, empty,

        where one ends and the other

begins, because the gun must go off

as guests of their bodies.

Working for My Father

Hercules, *one of the old constellations, called ἐνγονασιν*
by Aratus, Hyginus, and Ptolemy, and described by the
first as "a figure like that of a man in sorrow."

—The Penny Cyclopaedia

Two animals straddled the Columbus highway

and remained there while I worked
for my father—mailing invitations, updating

the computer. Each animal died intangibly,
        having crossed the onramp on separate

occasions—one moving east, the other
west—victims of their passing from one

        wood to the next. It was cold and
I wanted to say something about roadkill

so I said, "There's another deer," as we passed.
"That was a raccoon," he corrected, "too

small to be a deer." The Mercedes pitched
    into traffic and pressed me expensively.

        ⦀

The Midwest collects birches, freezes
them, and listens as they split in distant ice.

At night dreams grow four legs and confront
one another, some move through and

some get stuck listening when the ice
takes them, some stand in headlights.

        ⦀

The following morning the deer was wreathed
in obvious burial snow.

        "The deer's still there," I said,
"I wonder when they'll take it away."

Facing me he said, "A deer is like a horse, a raccoon
is more like a dog. Stop being metaphorical."

        ⦀

Hercules once had to learn humility
by chasing a red deer, a deer he could not kill,

and the deer was mine, its antlers tangled
in kite string as the kite rose above the trees, pulling

as the sky pulled back. I lunged and missed
for years.

⫴

When I last saw the roadside deer, so
small, I passed with the hope

to find my own way out—should I lie there,
broken—a beast on whatever road I was at.

⫴

Returning to California in spring, I held
the phone close to my ear; his voice,

far away, said, "The thaw came early, and you know
what? That deer was still on the side of the road,

the one that I never saw." I hesitated.
He continued, "I was looking at the raccoon

on the other side because I was looking
at you. You must have been looking at me."

The Park Below

Branches of this tree

are of the human kind,
wooden gloves and hardly

     a leaf.

And there is something
of my wife in it,

how timid

she can be with words,
     and wood

in the timbre of her voice.
She is also

a quaking aspen—tall,
freckled, an angle

true with the land
beyond spectrum. I fail

to understand each
movement's spray, each

bell's syllable.

Perhaps the affliction
            is mine,

how my words come
and never   take root,

how quickly I pass
to inadequate echo. A home

built from that wood
is easy against wind, the moods

of season. I take
                  her branches

by hand. I'm
silenced and shown how

to speak.

We Lost the *Avant-Garde* to Mass Culture

This morning's headache had the glare
of an empty bowl—
   but the birds were at

the water, the sun was steep at the edges
  of the window as I reached for a box

of Cheerios,
  I poured to the very end and nothing,

     I reached the powder.

Are you going to test me today? I asked. But
there was one left,
    a single *O* wandering the box,

   and I watched it—
it crept unfeeling about its predicament, it

   echoed with predictability—

    tiny spherical, lodged in a corner, and
   going where the box would go—

a tilting, rattling thing. I placed myself
     within the hole for an hour.

Bolero

It was 1979. There were a few orange tree orchards left
in Orange County. John Lennon lived. I was careful
like the mole digging up the front yard. I emerged
from the dark hallway, barefoot, it was Sunday,
I turned on the TV and was careful to mute the sound.
And I believe you have never seen Bo Derek in a silent, empty
living room grow bright from a warming cathode
running along a Mexican beach, her one piece flesh
colored swimsuit against oiled, sun-marked skin.
And I was careful, I was alone, I checked behind
me, looking for light from under a door, listening
for the squeal of a hinge. Then a motorist
lit up the front windows and drove on. I hit the off switch
and stood there, breathing hard, tingling like static
from the television discharge. I never learned
how others do it, but I learned to look at women privately
and in private, my eyes coming through a dark tunnel
to a throbbing kind of light, as out of a hole, the old
throbbing of analogue beauty unscrambling
in front of me, a terrifying pose. It was so strange how
afraid I was of getting caught. Of getting caught looking

at slow motion Bo Derek, at lounge chair Bo Derek,
piña colada Bo Derek emerging from the water. Afraid
of those beaded Mexican braids, staccato on her shoulders,
white sand at her feet, the salty swell of the gulf
pulsing on the sombrero end of the world. I was afraid for a long
time, a child of some in-between, and years would go by
before I could make any sense out of that sexual fear
that came from just looking and the thrill of just looking,
and years would go by before I watched Blake Edwards' *10*
again, watched Bo Derek in bed with Dudley Moore
while they played Ravel's *Bolero*, what Ravel mockingly called
"an orchestra without music," a piece that when first performed
had women falling from chairs while crying *Stop, stop I'm going mad!*
It was the indecency of the rhythm, the impropriety
of the tease, the long and overreaching crescendo, the lack
of a satisfactory tonal resolution that may explain
the great success of *Bolero* and the even greater success
of sex in the 1970s, it might even explain Dudley Moore's
nickname, "The Sex Thimble," or explain how I had searched
for something as frenetic and unattainable in my girlfriends
for so long, forcing each of them to run along the beach
in perverted judgment, wanting something that was incapable
of satisfying even the Sex Thimble in me. An orchestra
without music is sex without love, but how the orchestra
still plays whatever notes they're given, and they need to play
to finally understand what music is when and if it finds them.
And I can't help but see how all this made Bo Derek a sex icon,
and her perfect breasts would go on to be smothered in honey
and licked clean by young Arab men in later films. So
it happened when I was in bed with my wife for the first time
and she turned her back to me at the moment she removed

her blouse and bra, pulled my hands to her chest and said
that her breasts were small, and she would understand
if I didn't want to keep going. Because it never occurred
to me that sex could be such an act of courage, a raising
of a baton until the figure of brown hair pouring upon me
became the syncopated overture to the rest of my life.
And these were the greatest breasts I had ever seen. I asked
if she wanted to hear some music, I had just the thing.

Blazon for Our Time

Your bare legs make the symphony
so very dirty. You risk cliché when your hair

sweeps over the pillow unlike twilight

over a field. Your brain matter is woven sex in

what looks like a sweater. Your hands are little and
your hands are big. You towel yourself off

when you shower. You laugh and say
it isn't serious when you fall, when you push

the bicycle seven blocks with a warped rim

so it can be trued. I will not undo the expectations of
your breasts. They also float in rivers and

poke from egg shells. Your vagina has a lot

to say in a tone both furtive and alcoholic.
It falls asleep beside your forefinger.

You are pieces of atoms and entire
atoms in a mysterious terrarium of organs.

You are not a good singer except for

Cindy Lauper's "Time After Time," but then
you mess up the lyrics and look so well-made—

so much like your father, the undercover cop,
the Vietnam vet, the taskforce; or your biological

father named Randy Fisher who used to run
Ray Fisher's pharmacy, sold it and

disappeared. You are almost everything

about you: light hairs you wax
away, the creases on your knees like bitten

dough balls, and your fathers, whose absences
are everywhere on your back like the edge

of a map, whose shoulder blades are stiff

flags in heraldic vexillology, that coat of arms
blazoned with a girl unbuttoning a red

dress. You are the banner in the high breezes

that visited my sleep when I was a boy.
At night, when you kick the sheets and

sweat, you are this appropriate image.

When She's Writing

I listen at the door—
if Freud were here, he'd call this the *unheimlich*

and she would tell me to stop lurking
in the hallway where the mind's

pyramidal nerve tosses apples of love and apples
of discord. Let me in I say!

In a holy place, leave a token gesture behind
like a wrist watch or a ball point pen

the way tourists do on Emily Dickinson's grave.
Here is a grave

in a home, when she's
at it, a grave that is not of the home, and a husband

who forgets to eat and runs around the house all day
with a poem to share until

it is evening, until he hears footsteps
behind him and stops—

Who's there? I ask. "Me, Diogenes. Are you
an honest man?" And in his vow of poverty, in his
madness pushes a lantern

to reveal a face like a ghost ship, a wet
house. I reply, "I am everything

that ought to remain hidden."
Take me to live in a barrel in Athens and

teach me to be a cynical fool. For all
my weakness and nakedness, I am, you are, Zeus is

not my father. We are not of the home! We are
the uncanny and in every dark barrel of water

a kind glimmer. In the end, even Pound
was on to something. "If love be not

in the home, then there is nothing." But doesn't every man
lack symmetry, the apple split

into seeds and stars? I fall apart

at the silence when she's writing—

I drop an orange into ale, it's still early
so I wait.

Carried by a Bee

Sometimes my ass falls asleep
and it spreads like
                    forty black ships toward
Ithaca when I think of getting to something real
in a book. Tired
postures and self-inflicted

imperialism, half a life
under the guise of
                  "fearful childhood" with parents,
whose anger, so glorious, sprouted

glimmering wings.

      1.
      heretofore I am spooked as is

      and possibly forever

We are spooked of each other. We work
in the dark. Yeats writes,
"For arrogance and hatred are the Wares
Peddled in the Thoroughfares"
because he was too afraid of mistaking
politics with art—

of Maud Gonne, "It's certain that fine women eat
a crazy salad with their meat"

because she carried a gun and did not love him.

How traumatizing Yeats' youth had to be,
that certain Asperger's attention, that public
awkwardness, those dressed rehearsal dialogs
he wrote and memorized in case he needed to ask someone
directions to the British Library.

2.
I have a hunch the soul is, almost,

a rice net in a stream

On the school bus, boys

framed by heavy sliding windows, gesticulating
behind me. So

hard to forget
their haircuts—the mullet, the Mississippi top hat, the ape
drape, the business in the front

and party in the back, the Kentucky waterfall,
the Swedish Flokati rug—
so many tiny angry genitals, so much angry hair.

    3.
    I wonder where that anger comes from

    little boys and their yellow cheeks

Because fear and anger defines some of me, I want to say
the presence of love numbs it. I remember

one date I took Tana to a Greek restaurant
and she calmly pointed out

    "You have a bee on your neck."

She didn't know I also have a bee allergy, and that I might die
in the middle of the gyro,

but my next move was crucial: not to scream like a little
girl or flail about—

    I reached to my neck and held the bee
in my hand. I asked to be excused and

with mutual tenderness, we cradled each other
so we would not die. Since then

I sometimes feel the sting in moments of pleasure,
in the happiness when she comes to me

and carries me like the tremendous bee
I delivered to the parking lot, knowing at least I'd leave my life
in style, and from then on, whenever I hear

The Stone Roses' song "Made of Stone,"

    I feel the bee leave my hand.

    4.
    if we are not the victims of our own kind hearts then

    our stupid lives are sad

The Double Life of Veronique

At some point during the movie I felt
        a hand rest itself on my right

      leg which oddly belonged to the man
to my right, and who, without ceremony or suspense,

      without permission or cliché, was
lonely; who, like Veronique, had lost

his doppelganger due to some tragically frail
        disposition they both shared; whose

      other hand also needed a leg to touch
because, like the women in the film, I wanted

to believe the man's emotional twin had given everything
        to free them from what was destined to kill

      one or the other, and this is how the man
must grieve. When, in the hospital, Weronika

83

drags her coat on the white linoleum and
                we are pulled through the long, cold

     hallway, I imagine it's because love
has been too easy, and beauty's a debt

            as much as youth is, as much as her collapse
brings the audience to some fearless,

necessary understanding that we are together, we
        are watching, and we feel everything.

The Snow People

(Suddenly weather.)

Her breathing gathers, resembling fluff.

Trees drop everything to pose.
Love is gradual, a bottle

by sips, a bottle
poured onto the floor.

Winter coat,
I've come to depend   on you.

Snow comes,
the Chicago kind, barely Styrofoam,

barely water
stunned white.

(Suddenly Denver; suddenly
St. Louis.)

We're carved from cold:
                    the jeweler's panoptic diamonds
          now dust,

                    now ivory nerve, splinter, busted toe nail.
Branches scrawled in chalk, the city

          collecting lint. Love is cellophane salmon
                              fish markets, amber syrup

in silver tins. Desire changes
                    with altitude, rivers freeze,

                         iceships harden into coma.

          (Suddenly our teenage years
                    were fast-food, beer games, lumbering

sex on camera.) Marriage
                    is a chilly argument.

          The reckless classes
                    wait for dark, build fires, burn things.
                              But who are we? Consumers

out walking, boot prints pairing up, snow people
                    like charmed glass. What now

          but splendid shivering?

Notes

The Samuel Beckett quote from part 1 is taken from *Endgame.*

In "On the Isle of Erytheia," Erytheia is the island whereon Hercules completes his tenth labor by killing Geryon, the three-headed shepherd to a magnificent herd of red-skinned oxen.

The section quote by Lawson Fusao Inada is taken from "My Father and Myself Facing the Sun."

In "Slobs of the Ineffable Go to Evensong," Evensong is the Anglican liturgy where the Evening Prayer is mostly sung, and the line "the fall furthers the flight" is taken from George Herbert's "Easter Wings."

The phrase "odd bloom" in "The Odd Bloom of Sept. 11, Seen from Space" is taken from an interview with Astronaut Frank Culbertson on the tenth anniversary of September 11.

The Samuel Taylor Coleridge quote from part 2 is taken from *Religious Musings: A Desultory Poem, Written on Christmas Eve, in the Year of Our Lord, 1794.*

In "These Arrow-Smitten Stymphalian Birds," the birds are a reference to the sixth labor that Hercules completes by using a musical rattle to scatter the birds before shooting them out of the sky.

The section quote by T. W. Higginson is taken from *Oldport Days*, 1873.

In "Working for My Father," the deer references Hercules' third labor, where he captures the Cerynitian Hind, a golden-horned deer, by mortally wounding it with an arrow despite promising not to kill it.

Iowa Poetry Prize and Edwin Ford Piper Poetry Award Winners

1987
Elton Glaser, *Tropical Depressions*
Michael Pettit, *Cardinal Points*

1988
Bill Knott, *Outremer*
Mary Ruefle, *The Adamant*

1989
Conrad Hilberry, *Sorting the Smoke*
Terese Svoboda, *Laughing Africa*

1990
Philip Dacey, *Night Shift at the Crucifix Factory*
Lynda Hull, *Star Ledger*

1991
Greg Pape, *Sunflower Facing the Sun*
Walter Pavlich, *Running near the End of the World*

1992
Lola Haskins, *Hunger*
Katherine Soniat, *A Shared Life*

1993
Tom Andrews, *The Hemophiliac's Motorcycle*
Michael Heffernan, *Love's Answer*
John Wood, *In Primary Light*

1994
James McKean, *Tree of Heaven*
Bin Ramke, *Massacre of the Innocents*
Ed Roberson, *Voices Cast Out to Talk Us In*

1995
Ralph Burns, *Swamp Candles*
Maureen Seaton, *Furious Cooking*

1996
Pamela Alexander, *Inland*
Gary Gildner, *The Bunker in the Parsley Fields*
John Wood, *The Gates of the Elect Kingdom*

1997
Brendan Galvin, *Hotel Malabar*
Leslie Ullman, *Slow Work through Sand*

1998
Kathleen Peirce, *The Oval Hour*
Bin Ramke, *Wake*
Cole Swensen, *Try*

1999
Larissa Szporluk, *Isolato*
Liz Waldner, *A Point Is That Which Has No Part*

2000
Mary Leader, *The Penultimate Suitor*

2001
Joanna Goodman, *Trace of One*
Karen Volkman, *Spar*

2002
Lesle Lewis, *Small Boat*
Peter Jay Shippy, *Thieves' Latin*

2003
Michele Glazer, *Aggregate of Disturbances*
Dainis Hazners, *(some of) The Adventures of Carlyle, My Imaginary Friend*

2004
Megan Johnson, *The Waiting*
Susan Wheeler, *Ledger*

2005
Emily Rosko, *Raw Goods Inventory*
Joshua Marie Wilkinson, *Lug Your Careless Body out of the Careful Dusk*

2006
Elizabeth Hughey, *Sunday Houses the Sunday House*
Sarah Vap, *American Spikenard*

2008
Andrew Michael Roberts, *something has to happen next*
Zach Savich, *Full Catastrophe Living*

2009
Samuel Amadon, *Like a Sea*
Molly Brodak, *A Little Middle of the Night*

2010
Julie Hanson, *Unbeknownst*
L. S. Klatt, *Cloud of Ink*

2011
Joseph Campana, *Natural Selections*
Kerri Webster, *Grand & Arsenal*

2012
Stephanie Pippin, *The Messenger*

2013
Eric Linsker, *La Far*
Alexandria Peary, *Control Bird Alt Delete*

2014
JoEllen Kwiatek, *Study for Necessity*

2015
John Blair, *Playful Song Called Beautiful*
Lindsay Tigue, *System of Ghosts*

2016
Adam Giannelli, *Tremulous Hinge*
Timothy Daniel Welch, *Odd Bloom Seen from Space*